SACAJAWEA OF THE SHOSHONE

By Natasha Yim | Illustrated by Albert Nguyen

goosebottombooks

© **2012 Goosebottom Books LLC**
All rights reserved

Series editor **Shirin Yim Bridges**
Editor **Amy Novesky**
Copy editor **Jennifer Fry**
Editorial assistant **Ann Edwards**
Book design **Jay Mladjenovic**

Typeset in Ringbearer and Volkswagen
Illustrations rendered in pen and watercolor

Manufactured in Malaysia

Library of Congress PCN 2011941875

ISBN: 978-0-9845098-6-7

First Edition   10 9 8 7 6 5 4 3 2 1

Goosebottom Books LLC
710 Portofino Lane, Foster City, CA 94404

www.goosebottombooks.com

The Thinking Girl's Treasury of Real Princesses

Hatshepsut of Egypt

Artemisia of Caria

Sorghaghtani of Mongolia

Qutlugh Terkan Khatun of Kirman

Isabella of Castile

Nur Jahan of India

Sacajawea of the Shoshone

To my editor Amy and publisher Shirin,
for their infinite wisdom and for making me a "goose."

~ Natasha Yim ~

SACAJAWEA OF THE SHOSHONE

Clouds of dust swirled across the plains, kicked up by galloping horses. Screams shattered the autumn air. Arrows arced across the crisp blue sky, sprung from Shoshone bows—but they were no match for the Hidatsa warriors' guns. Through the smoke of musket fire, Sacajawea saw men fall. Her heart thudded against her chest. She raced over brush and brambles, the berries she had been picking scattering around her feet. If she could cross the river, she might be able to get away. One minute, her legs churned against the swift current, the next, a pair of muscular arms scooped her up, carrying Sacajawea far away from her tribe and family—and into history.

Where she lived

1 *Sacajawea's tribe, the Northern Shoshone, were nomadic. They lived in tepees, which could be set up and broken down in thirty minutes.*

2 *After Sacajawea's marriage, she lived in a tepee outside the Mandan village.*

3 *On her journey west with Lewis and Clark, Sacajawea, Pomp, and Charbonneau shared a tepee with the captains.*

Columbia River

3

Great Falls
Three Forks

Nez Perce

2 **Mandan Village**

1 Shoshone

Yellowstone River

Snake River

Missouri River

Spanish Territory

Louisiana Purchase

When she lived

This timeline shows when the other princesses in The Thinking Girl's Treasury of Real Princesses once lived.

1500BC	500BC	1200AD	1300AD	1400AD	1600AD	1800AD
Hatshepsut of Egypt	Artemisia of Caria	Sorghaghtani of Mongolia	Qutlugh Terkan Khatun	Isabella of Castile	Nur Jahan of India	Sacajawea

HER STORY

Sacajawea was born around 1788 near the Salmon River in Idaho. She was the daughter of the chief of the Agadika band of the Shoshone. The Shoshone were a nomadic tribe. They did not stay in one spot, but moved from place to place in search of food. In the spring, they traveled west to the Camas Valley to dig for the bulbs of the blue-flowered Camas Lily, which they ate boiled or steamed. In the summer, they remained high in their mountain village, fishing for salmon in the rivers and feasting on deer and mountain sheep. In the fall, they hunted buffalo at Three Forks in Montana, where the Jefferson, Madison, and Gallatin Rivers converged.

She was called what?!

How did Sacajawea spell her name? What did it mean? Over time, it's been spelled Sahkahgahweeah, Sahcagahweah, even Tsakahkahweeah. Lewis and Clark never spelled it the same way twice in their journals. Some say her given name in Shoshone was Huichi, meaning Little Bird, and that the Hidatsa gave her the name SakaakaWiiya, later phonetically spelled (spelled as it sounds) Sacagawea, meaning Bird Woman. Today, the Shoshone tribe prefers the spelling of Sacajawea. In Shoshone, the word means, "a burden that is pulled or carried."

The Shoshone needed buffalo for meat, clothing, and shelter. But the annual buffalo hunt was a dangerous time for Sacajawea and her people. While the Shoshone hunters stalked buffalo, the Hidatsa tribe stalked the Shoshone. The Shoshone were known for their beautiful horses, and the Hidatsa often waited until Sacajawea's tribe came down from their mountain hideout to steal them. Often they would also capture Shoshone women and children to use as slaves.

When Sacajawea was about eleven, she helped her mother load their buffalo-hide tepee and cooking utensils onto a *travois*, or sled, and trekked for miles to the buffalo hunting grounds. It was here that Sacajawea's life changed forever. While she and the women picked berries in the woods, Hidatsa raiders attacked on horseback, killing Shoshone men, women, and children, including Sacajawea's mother. They seized Sacajawea, spiriting her to the Hidatsa village over 500 miles away. Except for her older brother, Cameahwait, she would never see her family again.

Her new surroundings along the banks of the Missouri River in North Dakota must have been very strange to Sacajawea. Instead of majestic mountains and sprawling valleys, a flat grassy plain spread out before her. Instead of tepee homes of willow poles and buffalo hides that could be quickly broken down, the Hidatsa lived in round, earthen lodges permanently set into the ground. Built of mud and grass, they were so large that several families, including their dogs and horses, could live in them!

Sacajawea could no longer freely roam the woods or fish the rivers of her mountain home. She was now a slave and had to work very hard. Many of her duties were not unlike those she had learned at home: caring for the children, drying meat, tanning hides, sewing clothes and moccasins, cooking, preparing furs for blankets, and gathering firewood. But unlike the Shoshone who traveled to find food, the Hidatsa grew sunflowers, pumpkins, tobacco, beans, corn, and squash. Sacajawea had to learn how to tend the fields, weed and dry vegetables, and grind corn into cornmeal. In time, she learned to speak Hidatsa, which was to play an important role in her life.

▲ *The Missouri River in North Dakota, Sacajawea's new home.*

▲ *Sacajawea must have missed the majestic mountains of Idaho.*

6

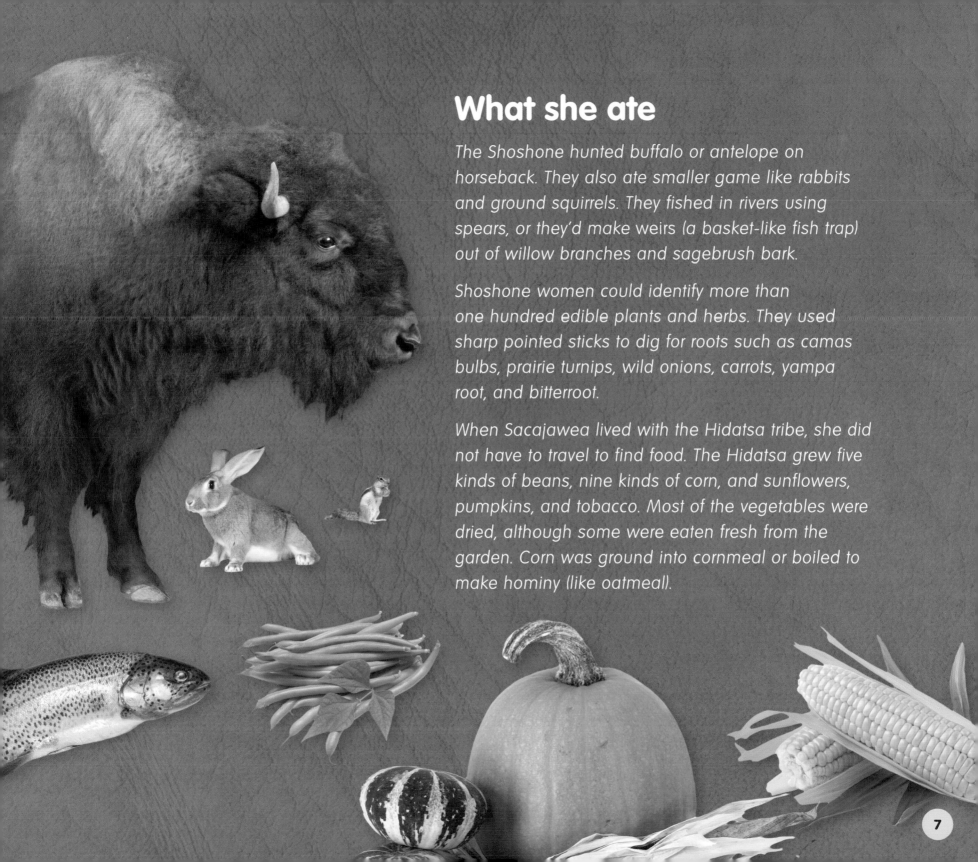

What she ate

The Shoshone hunted buffalo or antelope on horseback. They also ate smaller game like rabbits and ground squirrels. They fished in rivers using spears, or they'd make weirs (a basket-like fish trap) out of willow branches and sagebrush bark.

Shoshone women could identify more than one hundred edible plants and herbs. They used sharp pointed sticks to dig for roots such as camas bulbs, prairie turnips, wild onions, carrots, yampa root, and bitterroot.

When Sacajawea lived with the Hidatsa tribe, she did not have to travel to find food. The Hidatsa grew five kinds of beans, nine kinds of corn, and sunflowers, pumpkins, and tobacco. Most of the vegetables were dried, although some were eaten fresh from the garden. Corn was ground into cornmeal or boiled to make hominy (like oatmeal).

When she was fifteen, Sacajawea found herself thrust into marriage with a scruffy French-Canadian fur-trapper three times her age named Toussaint Charbonneau. At that time, it was common for Native American girls to be married in their teens, and to men much older than themselves. Charbonneau had lived among the Mandan, neighbors of the Hidatsa, for many years. The two tribes lived on opposite banks of the Missouri River and often visited each other's villages to trade goods.

It is thought that Charbonneau either bought Sacajawea from the Hidatsa or won her in a gambling game. In either case, he already had another Shoshone wife, Otter Woman. It was also common at that time in Native American culture for a man to have more than one wife, and Charbonneau adopted this practice. Although Charbonneau was probably not someone Sacajawea would have chosen for herself, she made the best of things and settled into the routines of a dutiful wife.

▲ *This painting, The Trapper's Bride by Alfred Jacob Miller, shows a similar marriage between a young Native American girl and a fur-trapper. However, this girl was lucky enough to marry someone closer to her own age!*

Sacajawea and her new family made their home in a tepee outside the Mandan village. She certainly must have preferred this, a reminder of her childhood, to the earthen huts of the Mandan and Hidatsa. And she must have been glad to have had another Shoshone woman to help share the household chores, and to speak to in her own language.

▲ *Shoshone tepees. This photograph was taken sometime between 1880 and 1910.*

▲ *An earthen lodge like the one that Sacajawea must have lived in as a slave.*

But, if Sacajawea thought she would live out her life quietly tending crops, cooking game, and raising babies, she was wrong. One November day in 1804, less than a year after her marriage, soldiers arrived at the Mandan village. Led by Captains Meriwether Lewis and William Clark, they were called the Corps of Discovery and they were on a mission. The President of the United States, Thomas Jefferson, had sent them to learn as much as possible about the 820,000 square miles of land he had just bought from the French. Much of this was unfamiliar territory to the white man. Jefferson wanted Lewis and Clark to look for trade routes, make maps, record the languages and customs of the native tribes in the area, and document the plants, rocks, and animals they found along the way. He hoped that they would also find a waterway along the Missouri River all the way to the Pacific Ocean.

▲ President Thomas Jefferson, the driving force behind the expedition.

◄ Captains Meriwether Lewis and William Clark, leaders of the Corps of Discovery.

© NOAA

▲ The red line tracks the Corps of Discovery's astounding journey across America and back.

◄ This mural, painted in the Oregon State Capitol rotunda, shows the Corps at the Celilo Falls on their way to the Pacific.

Why Sacajawea?

Toussaint Charbonneau had two Shoshone-speaking wives: Sacajawea and Otter Woman. When she met Lewis and Clark, Sacajawea was sixteen years old and pregnant. Why did Lewis and Clark choose Sacajawea to go along on the trip? Wouldn't it have been easier to travel without a newborn baby? One reason could be that Sacajawea was a Northern Shoshone whose tribe lived at the foot of the Rocky Mountains, whereas Otter Woman was a Wind River or Eastern Shoshone, whose territory was the valleys of Western Wyoming. The captains may have chosen to take Sacajawea because she would have been more familiar with the layout of the land around the Rockies, where their route lay.

The Mandan told Lewis and Clark that they would have to cross the "Shining" (Rocky) Mountains to reach the "Big Water" in the west. They would need horses. The Shoshone, Sacajawea's people, who lived near the Shining Mountains, were known for their beautiful horses. Captains Lewis and Clark would need someone who spoke their language. Charbonneau, Sacajawea's husband, had been hired as the expedition's guide. However, he only spoke Hidatsa, not Shoshone. But he did have two Shoshone-speaking wives.

© North Wind Picture Archives

Sacajawea's knowledge of both Shoshone and Hidatsa would indeed have been very useful on such a journey. But she was seven months pregnant and about to have a baby. No one really knows why the men decided to take Sacajawea instead of Otter Woman, Charbonneau's other wife, but this decision would ultimately make Sacajawea one of the most famous women in American history.

The Corps of Discovery decided to wait out the harsh North Dakota winter and leave in the spring when the ice thawed on the Missouri River. They built a shelter out of cottonwood trees. On February 11, 1805, Sacajawea gave birth to a healthy baby boy, Jean-Baptiste Charbonneau, whom William Clark nicknamed Pomp.

In April, Sacajawea bundled two-month-old Pomp into a basket and settled him on the bottom of a *pirogue*, a flat-bottomed boat. The explorers were on their way! They paddled westward up the Missouri River. Lewis and Clark would take turns exploring the area by water and on land. When Clark strolled along the shore, Sacajawea often walked with him, Pomp strapped to a cradleboard on her back. Clark documented the wildlife and plant life he observed. Sacajawea gathered wild artichokes, licorice, and a root called "white apple" for their meals. They became friends and Clark developed a great fondness for Sacajawea's son.

▲ *A woodcut showing the Corps building their winter shelter. This and many of the images that follow were original illustrations in a book,* A Journal of the Voyages and Travels of a Corps of Discovery, *by Peter Gass, printed in 1810 while Sacajawea was still alive.*

In the evenings, Sacajawea sat beneath the brilliant stars, dining on rabbit, beaver, and other game the men were able to catch. Sometimes after supper, to Sacajawea's amusement, the men stamped their feet to lively fiddle tunes.

Sacajawea was extremely helpful to the expedition. She helped to set up and break down camp, gathered firewood and edible plants and roots, hauled water from the river, and sewed clothing, all while taking care of her baby. Sacajawea also acted as a goodwill ambassador—a symbol of peace. The Native Americans who looked upon this bedraggled group of explorers with suspicion relaxed when they saw Sacajawea with Pomp on her back. No war party would travel with a woman and a baby!

▲ *Lewis and Clark's expedition diary, and a*
◄ *page showing William Clark's sketch of a*
"cock of the plains."

Her husband, Charbonneau, was a decent hunter, trapper, and guide who helped provide food for the Corps. But the men found him crude and arrogant. He did not treat Sacajawea well, often shouting at her, sometimes even hitting her. He was also, by all accounts, a coward.

One day, a violent gust of wind tipped the pirogue carrying Sacajawea and her family. Fortunately, the boat didn't capsize, but it quickly filled with water. Important papers, books, instruments, medicines, and trading goods started to float away. Sacajawea, clutching her baby, calmly scooped them up, saving everything except for some medicines, gunpowder, and garden seeds. Without her quick thinking, the expedition would have had to turn back. On the other hand, Charbonneau, who was at the helm, was so immobilized by fear, he was only spurred to action when one of the men shouted that he would shoot him if he didn't right the boat!

Exploring untamed territory was tough work. The stiff currents of the Missouri River made rowing difficult at times, and the Corps had to get out and push the boats from behind. Sometimes they'd pull the boats along with ropes from shore. Thick undergrowth on land had to be hacked away. Sharp rocks ripped holes in their moccasins. Sacajawea must have sewn hundreds of replacement moccasins along the way. The expedition could also be dangerous. The Corps was almost swept away by a flash flood. They battled snowdrifts and near-starvation. While hunting, Lewis and Clark were chased by bears, wolverines, and bull buffaloes.

Captain Clark and his men shooting Bears.

An American having struck a Bear but not killed him, escapes into a Tree.

As they neared Shoshone territory, Sacajawea began to recognize familiar sights: the prickly pear cacti and wild cucumbers peppering the meadows that lay in the shadows of the Rocky Mountains; a rock that looked like a beaver's head rising out of the water. These were the Shoshone's buffalo hunting grounds. Six years ago, this was where Sacajawea had been taken from her people.

Imagine the joy and amazement that greeted Sacajawea when she and the Corps of Discovery finally arrived at the Shoshone camp. No one had known what had happened to her after she was taken by the Hidatsa. And now she was among her people again, alive and well and with a new baby!

There was an even bigger surprise in store for Sacajawea. When she entered the council tent to interpret for Lewis and Clark, the Shoshone chief, looking regal in his ermine cape with shell-studded collar, was none other than her own brother, Cameahwait! Sacajawea learned that her father, sister, and younger brother had died during the time that she was away, and that Cameahwait was the only family member she had left. Sacajawea ran to him, threw a blanket over his shoulders—a Shoshone gesture of love—and wept. Her joy was such that the meeting had to be stopped several times so she could compose herself.

Negotiating for horses to take the Corps over the Rocky Mountains was no easy task—everyone spoke a different language. So, Sacajawea had to translate Shoshone into Hidatsa for her husband, Charbonneau; Charbonneau translated Hidatsa into French for Private LaBiche; LaBiche translated French into English for Captains Lewis and Clark. In the end, Cameahwait agreed to sell them twenty-nine horses.

What she wore

Shoshone clothes were made of the hides of buffalo, elk, or other big game, or of woven fibers such as sagebrush or juniper bark.

In the cooler months, Shoshone women wore long, calf-length dresses with elbow-length sleeves, paired with leggings made of elk skins and fringed at the cuffs.

Dresses were tied at the waist and decorated with feathers, beads, and elk teeth. Belts and necklaces made of blue beads (very valuable to the Shoshone) were also worn.

Sacajawea once traded her precious blue beaded belt so that Captain Lewis could have an otter skin coat he really wanted. This would have been quite a sacrifice for her.

Most of the time, the Shoshone did not wear shoes; however, in cold weather or when traveling, they would don moccasins made of deer, elk, or buffalo hide.

As wonderful as it was to reunite with her people, Sacajawea chose not to stay, and she and her family continued their journey with Lewis and Clark. For almost three weeks, they trekked over the steep and icy terrain of the Bitterroot Mountain range, huddling against the bitter cold, rain, and sleet. They didn't have much to eat except cornmeal and berries. There were no animals to hunt and they had to kill two of their horses for food.

▲ *This pen, ink, and pencil sketch made by Charles M. Russell in 1918 shows an almost-frozen Corps of Discovery.*

Half starved, Sacajawea and the Corps of Discovery finally emerged onto the beautiful sun-drenched Weippe Prairie, land of the friendly Nez Perce. There, they gorged on salmon and berries. The explorers stayed with the Nez Perce for about two weeks, collecting food and building boats for their journey onward.

Finally, the expedition resumed its travels down the Clearwater River. In November, seven months after Sacajawea first set off from Fort Mandan, she finally heard the roar and crash of the ocean. But powerful waves made it impossible to get any closer to the sea along their water route. They had to make camp inland. They built a fort in a protective grove of pine trees, and sheltered there through the damp, gloomy days of winter.

One day, a local tribe arrived with blubber from a whale that had washed up on the beach. Lewis and Clark thought it was delicious and formed a small group to see the "Big Fish" and get some more blubber. Sacajawea wasn't included. As you can imagine, she was really upset. She had come such a long way and she still hadn't seen the "Big Water"! She wanted to see the "Big Fish," too! The captains finally agreed, and Sacajawea made the five-day trek with Pomp to the Pacific.

There are no records of Sacajawea's reaction, but it must have taken her breath away to see the wide expanse of water stretching for miles to the horizon and to finally breathe the salt-laced air. The sight of that immense whale, the largest animal any of them had ever seen, must also have struck her with awe and wonder.

While at the shore, the captains searched for trading vessels to carry the message back to President Jefferson that they had made it all the way to the Pacific Ocean. They never saw one. The president would have to wait until their return to get the good news.

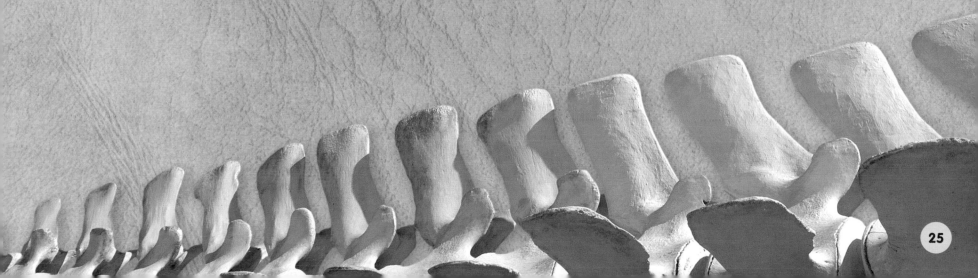

In March of 1806, Sacajawea and the Corps of Discovery turned around and headed back, arriving at the Mandan village one year and four months after they had left it. Clark, who was very fond of Pomp, offered to adopt and educate him. Sacajawea and Charbonneau wanted to wait until he was older. When Pomp was four, Sacajawea and Charbonneau made the journey to Clark's hometown of St. Louis, Missouri.

Sacajawea's husband took up farming and the family stayed in St. Louis for two years. In the end, though, Charbonneau preferred living among the Native Americans in the rugged Wild West to being a farmer. And so, in the spring of 1812, he and Sacajawea left Pomp to be brought up by William Clark, and journeyed west with a fur-trading expedition. They wintered at Fort Manuel in South Dakota. There, Sacajawea gave birth to a baby girl, Lizette. Many believe that Sacajawea then succumbed to "putrid fever" (typhus) and died a few months later. She would only have been about twenty-five years old.

▲ St. Louis was a growing industrial city in the time that Pomp knew it. This old photograph shows the Eads Bridge being built over the Mississippi River. It was completed in 1874. Pomp died in 1866.

◀ Pomp's friend, Duke Friedrich Paul Wilhelm of Wurttemberg, was an explorer who went looking for the sources of the Missouri and Mississippi Rivers. William Clark may have introduced him to Pomp.

What happened to little Pomp?

When Sacajawea and her husband returned west, they left Jean-Baptiste with William Clark, who had promised to provide him with a good education.

When he was eighteen, Jean-Baptiste met a German duke named Paul Wilhelm who took him to Europe. Pomp traveled around Europe for six years studying art, literature, and music. He could speak English, French, German, Spanish, and several Native American languages.

Despite his excellent education, Jean-Baptiste preferred living in the wilderness like his father, and became a fur-trapper, trader, and interpreter. Later, he moved to California and was the mayor of Mission San Luis Rey for a time. He also mined during the gold rush.

At sixty-one, Jean-Baptiste went to Montana to look for gold. He became ill, possibly from pneumonia, and died on the trail near Jordan Valley, Oregon.

Nobody really knows what happened to Lizette Charbonneau. It is believed she died in infancy.

Dedicated in the memory of
BAPTISTE CHARBONNEAU
Papoose of the
LEWIS and CLARK
EXPEDITION 1805 - 1806
SON OF
SACAJAWEA
Born Feb 11 1805

From her mountain home to the banks of the Missouri River, over the majestic Rockies to the pounding waves of the Pacific, Sacajawea had traveled farther than any American woman of her time. She had survived an almost disastrous boating accident, a flash flood, bitter cold, inhospitable terrain, illness, and near-starvation. She had endured all of this with remarkable placidness and cheerfulness, as several of the Corps noted with admiration in their journals.

Today, there are three mountains, two lakes, and twenty-three monuments named after Sacajawea, and her likeness appears on United States stamps and coins—a testament to this adventurous teenager's contribution to Lewis and Clark's exploration of the American West.

Bibliography

Berne, Emma Carlson. *Sacagawea: Crossing the Continent with Lewis & Clark*. Sterling, 2010.

Bial, Raymond. *The Shoshone*. Marshall Cavendish Children's Books, 2001.

Clark, Ella E., and Margot Edmonds. *Sacagawea of the Lewis and Clark Expedition*. University of California Press, 1983.

Dekeyser, Stacy. *Sacagawea*. Franklin Watts, 2004.

Lewis & Clark's Historic Trail. http://www.lewisclark.net/index.html.

National Park Service. "*Sacagawea*." http://www.nps.gov/lecl/historyculture/sacagawea.htm.

PBS. "*Sacagawea*." http://www.pbs.org/lewisandclark/inside/saca.html.

Rowland, Della. *The Story of Sacagawea: Guide to Lewis and Clark*. Yearling, 1989.

Schneider, Mary Jane. *The Hidatsa*. Chelsea House Publishers, 1988.

Sutcliffe, Jane. *Sacagawea*. Lerner Publications, 2009.

The Lewis and Clark Trail. http://www.lewisandclarktrail.com/.

The Shoshone Indians. http://www.shoshoneindian.com/default.htm.

Woodward, Tim. "Sacajawea." *The Idaho Statesman*. http://sacajawea.idahostatesman.com/index.htm.